VietNam
...again
...and again

Michael R Martin

VietNam Again and Again!
Copyright © 2020 Michael Ray Martin

All Rights Reserved. This book or any portion thereof may not be reproduced or used in any manner whatsoever without the express written permission of the publisher (except for the use of brief quotations in a book review)

Michael R Martin Publishing LLC
P.O. Box 67331
Topeka, KS 66667
mm900835@gmail.com

ISBN 978-0-578-67167-3 (paperback)
978-1-7349770-0-4 (ebook)

First Printing 2020

Table of Contents

Introduction. ix
Dedication. xiii

PART ONE: War & Weapons

1970. 2
Our World. 3
The Younger Ones. 4
A Hundred and One. 5
Look Homeward Angel 6
Land. 8
Wish. 9
THE BOMBS! 10
the Other Children 12
CLEAN GLEAMS 13
Flying Bullets on Path 14
An Unknown Soldier 15
Armed to the Teeth 16
Spectre. 19
Shaking Courage 21
Sapper–My First Patrol 23
Runner in the Fence Line 25
their Valley of Death. .28
WAR 33
Born An American. 34

Ah, Canada! 35

Peace 37

Peace Talks. 38

Cease Fire Supervisory Council–2/16/1975 39

Visions of Paranoia 40

Green Berets. 42

PART TWO: Politics & History of War

Monday October 28–Veterans Day 46

When You're in The Military 47

A Barrack's Cell 48

Stuff 51

An Earth Burnt Black 52

Imagining 54

Doomed 56

Nixon Administration 57

JFK and LBJ. 59

Of Legislators and Fools 64

Grieving Widows 65

PART THREE: Personal Matters

The Fool On The Hill 70

Electric Brains 71

Motorcycle Clock 72

Cruising the Drag 73

A Subconscious Mind 75

Used 76

Special Effects 78

Saying Goodbye 80

Families 81

TALK 82

Life Size 83
Gotta Be Near You All of the Time 84
Of Bushes and Bees 85
Your Breeze 86
Green Grass 87
Silent Atmosphere 88
Expecting Love 89
Treat You Right 90
One 91
21 December 1969 92
Far Away 94
By The Day 95
After Three Children 96
One Outlook 97

PART FOUR: Spiritual

Prehistoric 100
Heaven and Hell 102
This Thing Called Time 103
Chaffing of Beauty 104
Day and Night 105
Fog 106
The Retarded Children's Ward 107
At 21 109
A Mutual Thing 110
Behind the Back Talk 111
The Preacher 112
Forty Below 113
The Service Church Situation 1968 115
Off the Wall 117

PART FIVE: Nature's Beauty

Fall 120

Lake Shawnee 121

I am the Lake 123

A Horse 124

Trees Do 125

Empty Beer Can 126

Hey Flying Saucer 128

Polluted People Prosper 129

The Machine 130

PART SIX: Miscellaneous Musings

My Disobedience 134

Lites 135

Inner Light 136

Don't Care 137

Defiantly 138

I Ride the Wave 139

20 140

Wait 141

My Mother Said…. 142

Haircut 143

PART SEVEN: People & Characters

Sara Beth 146

John Wayne 147

W. C. Fields 148

Mother Goose 149

The One Armed Man of Alleyways Where 150

The Reporter 151

Apollo Eight 152

Of Feeling Low 153
Lonely Cliff 154

SUMMARY… AND IN THE END
In the Final Analysis 157
the long Black Wall 162

Introduction

THIS IS A BOOK OF poems that I wrote as a young man from my personal experiences of the late sixties and early seventies. Many other people lived thru this same time period and were also affected by the VietNam War and the politics of this era. The turbulent decade of the sixties saw emotions rise to fever pitch and as I wrote down most of these poems, I hoped they would help chronicle the history from a young person's view, as opposed to the older generation's view.

I have used great poetic license, including the use of many new words that I made up or modified of existing words; hoping to develop my own poetic sound or style. I know these new words may not survive outside of this book, but I enjoyed employing them and I hope maybe some of them will be found entertaining or humorous to you, the reader.

As a Topeka high school student in the late sixties, graduating in 1967 – I had time and was able to form my own opinions about the unfolding VietNam War. It was there everywhere before us, especially on the evening news; war reports of success and failure. It became obvious to me and many other young men and women, that the United States and our military were trying hard to fight a valiant, but yet, very limited guerrilla war in South East Asia to combat the expansion of communism.

We had been involved by our support of the French in what is called the first Vietnamese War for several years, but not with boots on the ground. Then, after the defeat of the French at the battle of Dien Ben Phu in 1954 – we became increasingly involved— and after the Gulf of Tonkin incident in 1964, we entered the war with boots on the ground to help the South Vietnamese government.

The French defeat by the Viet Minh communist revolutionaries under Ho Chi Minh could have been a learning experience; we could have learned from the history of the French failure. But, as often happens in politics—history began this morning— and arrogance of the egotistical moment overruled common sense. The need for real planning to ensure a favorable outcome over the communists in VietNam was placed on second burner and the thought of how could such a small and poor country possible cause the United States much trouble, became manifest.

At the time, I thought, as a patriotic young American that if the blood of nineteen-year-old men was to be shed, then, there should be an urgent and powerful plan to defeat the enemy and win the war. However, as the evening news illustrated on a daily basis – there was no recognizable strategic plan unfolding that would lead to a victory and an end to the war.

The Army's dead enemy body count figures became a mere smokescreen to cover up and obfuscate the stalemate and quagmire this war had evolved into. I kept asking myself, what is the value of one nineteen-year-old life? What is the value of each and every life lost in a war without any progress or conclusion?

By the time I graduated high school in 1967, I knew I didn't think this war was worth fighting, especially in such a limited and restrained manner. In 1967, almost everyone knew and rationalized that the VietNam War was a bloody, ill- thought out mess. To fight the spread of communism was a good and gallant endeavor, but if we were afraid to fight and win – why fight at all?

After graduation my draft induction date was set by the Army, corresponding to my nineteenth birthday. Fortunately, I was able to join the Air Force before my Army induction date arrived. I did this because I didn't believe in the manner in which this war was being waged and by now some twenty thousand plus soldiers had sacrificed their lives. After basic training, I was trained as a Security Policeman and eventually sent to a Thai Air Force base in South East Asia for the customary one-year tour of duty – from May of 1970 to May of 1971.

One of my first looks at the war up close was when we flew over South VietNam at night with all the explosions on the ground lighting up the night sky. Although I received Combat Security Police training, I would not be involved in any real combat or fire-fights during my year in Ubon, Thailand. I am grateful that I could serve my country for four years and still be able to ascertain and protect myself from what others could not – an illogical war. So many young men went to their death without fully comprehending what was being asked and demanded from them by political leaders who were unwilling and afraid to fight to win and most of whom never travelled to the war zone.

This book has poems about the war and weapons of war, about my political views, about the young loves of my life and anything that was on my mind during this time of my life. There are many poems that are meant to be humorous or just plain nonsense and others that may be hard to define – from the corners of my mind. My hat goes off to the real warriors of the VietNam War and I hope these poems may be of interest to the veterans of that time, the baby boomer generation, and all people of the post WWII and Korean War era.

I'm hoping that today many young Americans who have not had the prospect of being drafted or fighting in a war zone might look at the VietNam War and see heroes who fought for the freedom that they now enjoy – just like many of the VietNam Veterans looked upon the heroes of WWII and Korea and absorbed and found the honor of our country's history.

When all is said and done, only the Word of God does not change, or its meaning for us till the end of time. Someday there will be no need of weapons of war and those men who have started wars down and throughout history will meet their match and much, much more.

Dedication

FREEDOM IS NOT FREE AND I dedicate this book of poems to the men and women who fought in VietNam and all those support troops who served in the SouthEast Asia theater of operations. There are always two sides to every story, but I chose to honor all who served their country in the VietNam War and in surrounding countries such as Thailand and on the many Air Force bases and Naval ships in the region.

I pray for the souls of all the men and women and their families who lost their lives defending our nation in this war. And I also pray for all the wounded, all the Missing-In-Action soldiers, and every family member affected. As we all know and have been taught by Jesus: there is no greater sacrifice that a man can make than to give his life for his fellow man. And the VietNam War was an example of that; men trying to create freedom and dignity for other men and nations.

PART ONE
War & Weapons

1970

See the shimmering, unsteady light,
feel the breeze whipping dissent in the night,
taste the death of pride and military might,
hear possessions breaking people –
feel the mornings heartache,
smell the far-off fear,
these are the essence
of today's towering steeple....
far-off yet so near.

Our World

My mind is on the brink of catastrophe

And my body surrounded by a world of misery.
The streetlight is bright
And the hoodlum a savage sight,
Unfortunately, many a hoodlum
And political opportunist
Think in terms alike.
Who or what gives birth
To these men of war?
Why do they seek
To take peace and
Cast it so far away
And never give us a say?
You and I know it's true–
Our world is so powerful,
Our world is so cruel,
Where do we seek
To find such foolishness?

We've been given every Godly grace,
Yet we ignore our God's face
And my mind lingers still—
On the brink of catastrophe

The Younger Ones

We seek not to destroy the establishment,
Unless you say we may not be a part of it.
The Young see the need for a newer answer,
But we would rather
Experiment with
Love than
War!

A Hundred and One

One life or a hundred
Is the choice…
That is handed down by Hanoi
To America weekly, and our voice?
The one life is that of freedom
Of all that world wars stand for,
Of all that liberty has restored.

There seems no human choice
So none is made—
And there really is only one;
To fight to win
The all out war of no return.
A hundred bodies or more
Every week are burned
As the cost of war's filling urn,
It's surely no melting pot
Though it once stood for a lot.

Look Homeward Angel

Look homeward boy and
Sense your far-off country.
You want to be there,
You love your country
But it's here you are
In a war many a young men see.

But does your country
Love you, soldier boy?
Oh, sure they care
But then they just stare.
Another day, another death—
Another dead young soldier boy,
Bites the dust of a history
In this quest of illogical fighting,
At the devil's bequest— so distinctively
And in such a complex vicinity
Of friend and foe and rice paddy proximity.

The young are against this warrish role –
The old know no probable remedy –
The Generals have no clue
And wait and contemplate and tomorrow
Another dead....another wounded....
Another traumatized soldier boy
Is drug off the Viet Nam battlefield.
Come and fight young draftee:

You have no choice,
You are here by federal decree;
You've come out of a vote-less bowl,
You, you young nineteen year old soldier boy.

The older generation and politicians
Guide us to war with no discussion,
And no fatherly distinction
Between winning and losing and
Our sacrifice of total extinction.

Mr. Johnson—let us fight to win…
Take off our gloves and let us begin
To die for something and not for nothing—
Instead of holding and hiding your head
And making us win the same hill
Over and over and over again.
Mr. Johnson—are you so full of …
That you can't see where we've been?

Of no choice, a free American, how lucky.
To be born with liberty and sight
And a responsibility to fight.
Yet, someone must set this right….
Ah, yes, they do recognize you
Back home in bold print
They've your name in the daily.
And so it goes: one more dead
Again, and again and again.

Land

Everyone owns the land
Yet let no one mortal man
Call himself lord of the land –
For then and only then
We'd need no military hand.
The fight over land
Goes all the way back;

To Man and Dinosaurs alike
Who came to show their might.
Millions and millions more dead....
Oh, what a sight –

The bad guys in their delight,
Preaching communism is right.
Vanity and cruelty reign
We see it again and again.

China, Korea, and now VietNam
Oh, dear God, lend us a hand
Send us a land loveless man –

To guide us away from this vain, profane

And unrestrained theory of man....

Wish

Wish the men
And the lava phoenix of war
Would leave us be,
Leave us free.
Let us breathe without this insensitivity;
Renew our brains from this insanity.
Power, power, and more power—
Men elevate themselves above God,
Above his unsearchable mysteries
Of faith and love and simple kindness—
To murder, maim and call it soundness.
Another year of fear and terror all around us;
The children cry out and they will find us
In our boundless sin and invite Him in—
The one who made what is all around us.
His wrath is coming—if we don't stop
Such violence which will surely drown us.

THE BOMBS!

We've seen the bombs fall,
tumbling fire into things below—
destructing, killing, whatever is,
letting nothing live to die slow.
An F-100 Super Sabre, wing mounted,
triple ejector bomb rack
pours napalm from the dim heavens,
leaving people's bodies burnt black—
a young girl clothed only in burnt skin
running and screaming down the road,
trying to escape the evilness within.
An AC-130 armored gunship
rains bullets on the enemies' wet heads,
flying like a demon reaping blood
for what ought to be only said.
It is easy to say the bombs should fall,
for a politician who is far, far, away....
But does he understand and comprehend such
cavalier evilness from within,
the sin of omission killing again—

or the suffering of the women and children here,
emotionally starving and looking so thin.
These complicit sins are marked to fear
and the diminishing nature of life over death—
and therefore,
we must surely ask— why are we here?

As we watch them die and suffer everyday—
someone somewhere has to say:
This is not the true American way.

the Other Children

the people, they cry to me,
wondering how it came to be,
people living like dogs around a tree—
realizing not their negative severity.
The Children cry not at night
only when the Sun shines light,
portraying all the wrong of our day,
all the war begotten victim's way.
No one eats bugs these days,
everyone has a television—they say
a car, a home, a family way—
Still,

These people, they cry to me
not consciously, only hopefully.
Graciously knowing that
somehow I must see,
all the trash, the death,
the disease;
the things some people take
commonly.

Our leaders look and fail to completely see
and relate only to war's ordeal,
And still, the people and the Other Children
that most will not see, they cry most
overtly....

CLEAN GLEAMS

A brand new factory clean M-16
Sits proudly in the not-so-new gun rack,
With a dull gleam, not moving, not caring,
Just waiting to be fired by some country's man—
A weapon built to kill though meant to kill naught?
Like a man, it will almost shoot itself,
Especially if you stare hard enough,
With glorifying eyes and man's long lust…
This weapon is one you've simply got to trust.
It demands thoughts of war's very nature:
Gas operated, air cooled, nomenclature.
Good thing I didn't miss this lovely war
For I know…
Our despair seems to be moving powerfully,
But are we aware where?

To protect our fellow man is not a travesty—
Sometimes self-defense becomes a necessity
And we seek only the safety that such weapons
Of war….
Can bring along with the meaningful gleam,
Of these brand new factory clean M-16s.

Flying Bullets on Path

Horrible on his horrible machine,
man made me fly this dead way
and made me look into the eyes of his war
and see Hell as man's horrible machine.
Justify death and he has conquered all,
justify killing and he has freed mankind all
and mastered the purpose of faith and it all.

All the while….
young men bleed in the far-off night
praying to God to attack the horrible machine
to destroy what pre-man has re-reasoned for.
Somewhere, someone must surely care
enough to stop and alleviate—
the Devil's deadly lethal snare
of these bullets flying through the air.

Meanwhile,
man's horrible machine dreams up new bullets to fly
faithlessly through the horrible air
as I have flown, like a bullet through air…

An Unknown Soldier

An unknown soldier falls and dies, even today,
Torn by bullets of an AK-47 seven point six-two;
Another manipulated body gone back to clay.
Today's Unknown Soldier is truly unknown
And his young soul surely needs a heavenly home.

Why did he come to fight and die this way?
What did he ever do or say to cause this—anyway?
Yet he lies bleeding and no one shares his calamity—
The draft board identified a number not protected
And that's a story that isn't quite right....
But who will help this number, this night?

An unknown soldier falls and dies, even today,
But almost no one cares or dares to say
That he did not give his life right;
For America is mostly free and economically upright—
Besides, he wasn't any of your kin, right?

Another unknown soldier falls and dies, even today,
How many more will fight and die for the USA
And not be rewarded by a cause or near peace
Before we open our eyes and see…
So many young soldiers' lives cease?

Armed to the Teeth

Guard mount is over and we head out,
Leaving the armory with this weapon
And that weapon, leaving nothing out.

An M-148 over my shoulder,
A .38 caliber Combat Masterpiece
Mounted securely on my belt.

The powerful and brutal M-60
Machinegun carried beside me
With the extra barrel in a tan pouch.

The blowing sand is the enemy at hand....
We grab the ammo cans, 5.56 and 7.62
And don't forget the 40 MM grenades too.

We jump in the jeep to find our posts—
A canister of 40 MM grenades falls off
This jerky jeep and into the roadway.

I should have put it on the floor,
Now there's going to be hell to pay....as
The Armored Personnel Carrier is at bay.

This will be a huge explosion
And the death of us all—
Somehow the driver swerves away—and then relief.

We may live to see another day,
We're supposed to be killing the enemy
And not disposing of ourselves.

So now we arrive at my assigned mortar pit,
Add an 81MM mortar to my weapons kit—
Mount the M-60 on the edge of the bunker.

Load the M-16 with 20 rounds of 5.56 firepower,
Yank a cartridge into the chamber,
Safety on–ready for my finger.

Thank God we made it to our machinegun-mortar pit....
To defend and protect the people and airplanes behind—
Things that are always on the enemies' mind.

"Hamburger" my assigned Thai guard,
Talks the usual nonsense to me—
He likes "Lucky Strike" cigarettes more than me.

Quite an array of F-4 Phantom jets
Being loaded for another mission tonight,
AC-130s revving up their turboprops, out of sight

These machines of war and freedom
Need our diligent protection
From rockets, mortars, enemy projections.

Last night they came for the AC-130s,
Sappers with AKs and grenades sneaking thru the night—
Seeking our premier weapon of might.

As Airmen loaded the deadly weapons
Aboard the armored, computer aimed version—
Soon to be circling above the aggression.

Then came the black clad sappers—
Running, avoiding detection... .
Till a K-9 alerted their planned destruction.

Quickly chaos and confusion—
Radio transmissions flew thru the night air,
Alerts went out and bullets were everywhere.

And then four sappers lie dead,
Along with our German Sheppard
That they shot in the head.

One in the field lies dead by the K-9's friend;
Shot thru and thru again with revenge
By such a highly trained K-9's friend.

One blown apart on the perimeter fence....
He never saw, heard, or knew
The M-79 grenade round that touched his heart.

Two more lay dead on the tarmac edge
Where the M-60 jeep blew thru them, enough said;
We stopped such aggression that was in their head.

Tonight, we sit and pray for safety's sake
And watch and watch for another attack…
By these suicidal sappers of the Viet Cong.

We know they'll probably be back before long;
Bravery comes easy when you want to stay alive—
Freedom for the folks back home is what we strive.

Spectre

The armored Spectre gunships are again alive,
Flying high in the night sky above the Ho Chi Minh;
Bringing a balance to the strange war below.

Saving lives of American and South Vietnamese too—
There will never be a braver aircraft crew,
Than the men of the AC-130 whom we totally knew.

The rutted paths of the Ho Chi Minh Trail
Marked Laos like a jungle map full of sin—
Time and time again we bombed them asunder.

Spectre gunships left Cong supply trucks
Blown apart beneath the mud and rain
And slowed the death that was to come.

Their drivers had to be chained in, it was said,
Fearing when the AC-130s would come again—
Spectre Gunships fighting valiantly in the night.

Our most Formidable Adversary to North VietNam
Was such a sight with all her guns.
Displaying American military might
So powerful thru out this warrish
And Hell like night.

A godless enemy is hard to fight,
But our Airmen **knew** wrong from right
And threw their valor into the fight.

Our Guardian Angels watched over us at night
As brave Airmen flew over the valley of death….
Without any respite
Over and over and over again.

Shaking Courage

my finger is on the trigger,

my boots walking thru the field,
looking for sappers in the night,
in their black clothing,
holding their AK-47s tight.

the Sergeant tells us to go….
and so we load our M-16s
and chamber a round, ready to shoot,
nervous at first and shaking too—
wondering when, what and who.
knowing we're sitting ducks
walking in the night,
uncontrollable shaking and fear…
now is the time for the shaking to stop.

it must stop or we will die here,
it's taking my nerves over the top—
my body is shaking violently,
is killing such an illicit thought?

the mind identifies the equation—
we must remember why we're here,
put the fear out of here…for
we've come to fight communists in the night.

calm and cool, the body reacts,
there'll be no giving up my life

without a fight this very night and
in a millisecond fear turns to battle.

I must find my delight in killing those
who want to kill me this night,
otherwise there will be no morning light
for me or those behind me, sleeping silently,
out of sight.

the shaking stops quickly and courage appears
when you're in the middle of a fight—
get that sapper in your sights
or it might be your last moonlight.

Sapper–My First Patrol

Sapper on the base at night....

the sergeant comes to us,
a guard mount filled with fright—
first night on the base perimeter
at the war's height.
Now we're in the field
and spread fifty feet apart—

our sergeant yells "Squad forward!"…
Locked and loaded, safety off,
we proceed with some uncertainty,
mere sitting ducks walking forward.
Slowly, quaking, shaking in my boots
can't stop shaking—know I'm going to die.

This sapper won't let my image slide by—
shaking still, more each minute—I ask myself why?
Finally realizing that now is the time to fight,
might as well try to live my way out of this plight,
finger on the trigger — ready to shoot....
my eyes use night vision darting from side to side
to sense any enemy movement—or small glimpse
of a bad guy in a slithering, shadowy stance.

The selector on full auto—it's all real now—
this M-16 is no longer a firing line toy.
Suddenly....the shaking is gone completely,

no more shaking, shaking, soldier boy.
I might as well fight and die;
cowardice is not borne within me,
the shock of war has come and gone,
five minutes of shaking on this
first patrol
is over and it will not control me.

Kill I will and kill I must to protect
those who fly and fulfill our hope—
that someday, there will be
no more deadly sappers in the night;
In their black pajama jump suits,
wired with explosive charges on their vests;
not planning on living thru the night—
high on drugs to null their rational thought,
ghastly A-K 47s glued in their hands—
they've come to make a Ho Chi Minh stand.

Now I see them in my dreams only,
a sad story, but still a reality:
they could come again in my mind's
vast dark alley.

Runner in the Fence Line

Unseen, here he comes
running silently in between
the two fence lines.

Avoiding the trip-flares
he is hard to see
dark and to the left of me.

I see the armed jeep
coming toward me
on the perimeter road.

To bring me and my Thai guard
coffee and see if we are alert
in the middle of this night.

Two Security Police shinning
their spotlight out at the darkness
towards the fences and village huts.

Guard mount intelligence
says they're coming tonight
to hit the barracks within sight.

Still, there's no buildup
and no officer shedding light—
on the forecasted fight.

My machine gun bunker lies
ready and M-60 loaded
two M-16s are also ready to go.

I'm looking all about
vigilant to the night
at barbed wires fences 20 yards ahead.

My Thai guard is looking too
but not too concerned about
being attacked this very night.

Here comes the jeep
with its big spotlight lit
stopping in front of my post.

They're looking my way
now and not out at the night
where the sapper is now in sight.

I can see him now perfectly in the light
all crouched down like a stage actor might—
loaded weapon clutched in his hand.

The sapper is frozen in the spotlight
grasping his AK- 47 tightly,
hoping he won't be seen.

Quickly,
I grab my M-16 to shoot him down
worried by the off-base huts
and those Thai people around.

But the jeep is in between…
my bullet will have to wait
for the sake of the men in the jeep.

The sapper is frozen in the light,
quickly I run to tell my fellow defenders
there's a bad guy in sight,

Suddenly, he is running now
down the fence line
as the jeep pursues....

They follow him with the light
running for his very life—but
he slithers thru the outer fence.

No need for them to shoot
randomly into the night
at this sapper who is now out of sight.

He probed our defenses
and he somehow got away
but the men in the barracks will live…

To see another day
never knowing the danger
lurking so close this very night.

their Valley of Death

they come and walk the hallway,
they receive their bombing orders,
each night—they mount their F-4 Phantom Jets
and perform their on the ground pre-flights.

then,
they lift off into the night—
bombs, guns, missiles—armed to the might;
never knowing if they'll be back,
they set their lives on the line
for God, country and their fellow man,
fighting against this godless Communist man.

and then,
they give their ultimate sacrifice—
some shot down, some captured,
some dying and never returning:
no greater sacrifice can be determined.

and now,
we wonder aloud—where is he now?
F-4 Phantom jet with tail number 703
never returned this bleak night—
is he alive and in God's sight?
or has he gone into a new divide?
these young pilots can never hide….

captured,
a prisoner to be tortured alive

locked in a bamboo cage: scorned,
mocked, spit upon, mentally abused…
the recipient of Communist rage—
back home,
mourned by his family and friends,

now,
he must suffer this godless hate,
mistreated for maybe thousands of days....
as this calamity of errors drags on and on
with no courage or common sense
from our so-called back home—political elites.

even,
one young American life is too much to lose,
why can't those in control come to perceive?
if we are so forlorn, how can we proceed?
there is a North VietNam above the line
where our leaders are fearful of China
and what China did for North Korea.
but our leaders don't fear graciously
for our brave pilots and young soldiers;
who need to withdraw and be rescued
from this ghastly, unsightly and hideous plight.
for we are here just to fight as we might
and there is no resolve to be found
by our deaf and blind leaders
lounging so many shores away
from the danger they espouse
in such a limited way.

still,
and here and now,
only prayers to God can save our men
for now, Jesus is with them, sitting on the clouds,
watching over them when no one else really sees them—
fighting so gallantly, flying into danger so swiftly.
these young pilots walk with Him and know no fear
on the other side as they see firsthand
the location of 'the valley of the shadow of death'
and the violent void created by all this disorder!

yes, they,
these brave men have given their lives to destroy sin-
and God is there with His glory to take them in
and comfort the souls of such brave young pilots
who have more faith than most American men.

Ho Chi Minh reigns over his deathly power;
over peace and everything that makes people's
lives go so terribly sour.
once again, we try to succeed
and bring death to him, Ho Chi Minh,
sitting in his villainous power.

Ho Chi Minh comes at us again,
determined to kill and kill again—
he has no respect, even of his own men—
even when we kill many more of them.

casually,
he strikes down American power and resolve;

he comes to steal, kill and destroy…
aligned with the powers of darkness,
but who are we aligned with?
we debate and debate for whose sake?

so we try to fight right and do no harm
but harm now lives in the Hanoi Hilton
and in bamboo cages out in the jungle
and we are so humbled by our own self-control.

yet,
we let these pilots walk beneath the scripture
hanging above the door and on the wall
that will save their soul and defend us all…
but, where is our mighty power at their back?

still,
our leaders keep us in without a win,
this overly governed down fight
that had at once been about a growing Communist sin.
we fight not hard, our policies constrained by fear—

what meaning can one life have?
what value is there as lives are lost—
so indiscriminately?
we retreat not when we might surrender
to a logical and compassionate ending here!

Oh, dear…
this war has been such a terrible fight,
a non-communist Viet Nam is now

completely out of sight....
there will be no win over Ho Chi Minh
and no freedom for the people within.

WAR

There's a war today
Of no winning way,
A war to kill, to illustrate
A true quality of the minds' hate.
It's said no man wants war
But greedy leaders will crusade
Or why all the sanguinary carnage?
Hitler, Mao, Ho Chi Minh—
Evil men keep coming again and again—
Taking peace like it's not a sin.
I'm but one cast in my war role;
But someday as a worker of peace
We'll all reject what we know we must
And those bloodthirsty world leaders
Will know they have to hush.
We've had five and are in our sixth
Since the one of 1776,
War wins but war for a world sick.
Men will differ and men will fight,
But only one way will men
Live without war's strife—
To tolerate the beliefs of others,
To share love and the land, mutually,
And it takes everyone, not some—
Under Jesus and our Father
Is the only way such peace Will ever come....

Born An American

I strolled along and suddenly
Upon some inquisitive thought,
Not a thought of self-pity,
I began to feel how lucky
I am to be a free American.
Who could be more lucky?
A very hungry man of India
I might have been,
Or maybe a Russian
Taught with misguidance,
Or even a guinea pig
Forced to die for science.
How lucky I am
What millions would give
To in America live.

Ah, Canada!

Just wanna run away from here,
this crazy war has no answers
only daily deliberations and fear—
no one really running things here.

So easy to leave for Canada
and say goodbye to this nightmare.
many have gone and stay there,
I could do the same—Oh dear!

What would my dad say?
just another war protester gone astray,
too scared to fight and die for the USA—
such cowardice he has, most would say.

This war is an illogical concentration of thought,
toppled dominoes are not something I was taught.
How many more must fight and die
and lie wounded on the evening news?

Such a fanciful political war—
it resembles some kind of a whore;
then there's Brown and Root
and all those who are in cahoots.

Give us young Americans some sanity here,
a reason to make the most high sacrifice,
instead of protesting or taking the northern road
to a malcontent place of no reassuring hold.

We would require some leadership to emerge
so we can feel our death would add up
to a better place for all the rest of us;
I can't disgrace my dad or the U.S.

I'll join the fighting forces and hope
some intelligent minds will pursue
a different course in Viet Nam
where a man's life counts for
more than the temporal morning dew.

Peace

Talk of peace-
An impossibility?
Not the least.
A quiet world?
No, always a beast,
Not the least.
A world of love
With one Dove,
From Heaven above—
Not the least.
A brotherhood,
Or childhood?
Not the least.
Talk of war—
Is a known door,
Not the least.
The vain and
Most selfish heart,
The Hawkish part,
True, the least.
But will life cease?
Not the least?
Keep talking peace!

Peace Talks

Talks of unloving chatter
About what shape of table
Does it matter?
Here in God's stable
Where children are all about,
The shape of a table seems a divine matter.
As pettiness lingers, producing dead life batter,
These talks of peace don't reform but disable
The future of a world gone completely unstable.

The younger world thirsts for sanity
And a world with less calamity.
These talks of peace
About the shape of a table
Destroy our hopeful humanity.
So daily, we pray, for an end—
To this ungodly insanity,
To this atheistic atrocity,
Of meaningless words
By North Viet Nam's
Communist family…

Cease Fire Supervisory Council–2/16/1975

Another cease fire comes along....
then, there were 151 communist attacks—
but, what about the cease fire?
And people still die:
just a one more Viet Cong lie.

The list goes on and on....
an unarmed GI helicopter is shot
down to this blood soaked ground
and five more are wounded:
no one can keep the Viet Cong bound.

What we have here is just another day....
when no one can say when the killing might stop—
the Cease Fire Supervisory Council
can talk and quarrel all round about
but in South Viet Nam, bullets are still swirling all around.

What manner of men give expectations ....
that are meant to just be broken again?
We fight and die and die once again
while false cease fires are some form of sin—
to a young soldier in this dark night's bin.

Someday, we Americans will all go home....
to that faraway shore and the light of day
and no more cease fires of Satan's way:
a lie, a deception, an omission of truth
to believe the devil…has cost us our youth.

Visions of Paranoia

at the night bunker
to guard this perimeter
weapons trained with insensitivity

staying alert to movements
all around and in front of me
trying to avoid calamity

scared to look but
peeking quickly all about
leaving nothing out

it may have meant life
it could have been death
or a very last breath

scared not to look about
through the night's fright
having to shoot at a shadow's sight

back on target—a vision entrails not stopping—
still darting quickly
sight's paranoia making me sickly silly

to see everything is a must
though frightened to the teeth,
please where is my belief?

no way to slow my looking
to let anything be left out
it was bred in me quickly

keep looking, they may be out there
must protect those behind me
my eyes peer into darkness

seeking safety among the demons
they come to steal, kill and destroy
my eyes are forever beside me

another night, another threat
but we are still here and yet
there is no end till the morning light.

Green Berets

Here we Airmen come to receive mortar training,
those of us chosen after volunteering,
we come with an interest in defending
a base we now call home and we are unrelenting.

These Green Berets are men of distinction—
wounded horrifically, yet healed miraculously
they come to train us with specificity
on the manning of the 81mm mortar.

They are here on restricted duty to teach
us how to light up the sky during an attack
with illuminating rounds—so we can see
the communist sappers slithering in silently.

They also teach us to shoot explosive rounds
to neutralize an enemy winning at night
on what might be a very big fight;
sappers coming to kill our AC-130 gunships, our might.

These Green Berets remove their shirts
in the Southeast Asian super heat
and we can see their brave battle scars.. ..
a round hole in the front of their chest
a hellish wide hole in their backside .

Oh, how can it be that they even lived…
these three sergeants tell us of the firefights
whence their wounds proceeded from,
only God's guardian angels saved these men.

Now here among us younger Combat Security Police
we are humbled by their sacrifice and prowess
to defend our country…as we see their scars of war
and know they are so much braver than anyone we know.

These men are our heroes as they teach us the mathematics
of measuring grids and pinpointing the enemy's wet heads,
and now we go to celebrate just knowing these men,
who are vowing to join the jungle fight once again.

They drink hard and teach us to eat raw eggs, shells and all,
we'll never be Green Berets; our stature is not as tall—
such an example of a brotherhood of courage and honor
who are giving the Viet Cong such a strong battle cry.

So many have died and are dying every day
to protect our freedom and way of life—
why can't all see—that freedom is not free
and unity is the opposite of a quavering knee.

I'm glad we got to know these three
Green Berets, stouter than a great tree,
giving everything that we might be free;
no greater gift has a man than these three.

PART TWO
Politics & History of War

Monday October 28–Veterans Day

Palmdale is such a nice soft name,
who'd ever guess what they suggest
to build the first of the worst.

Rockwell's International Assembly
churns out metal figures of strength
to soar high above a sunny desert.

Integrity, security, ceremonious pomp,
here comes the needle-nosed, swept wing thing
full of beauty, tantamount to future buffs.

John P. Brown threw himself down
upon Rockwell's desert ground
in the path of the very first B-1 Bomber.

Thousands there were for and one against—
who'd ever guess what this suggests;
a luring of apathetic nonsense?

To preserve our freedom, might be heaven sent,
although there are voices of dissent…
blessed are the peacemakers who invent.

When You're in The Military

When you're in the military....
No identity do you carry,
Dress is uniform and hair cut,
To kill the enemy is your sole cult.

When you're in the military ....
You think of serving your country
And your country shafts you sour
With KP, little sleep and long hours;
But discipline is what it is all about.

When you're in the military....
All you can fantasize thru
Is getting the hell out—
But all is fair in love and war
And the military, even from afar.

When you're in the military ....
Your rights are knocked away
And but a few remain to stay.

When you're in the military....
Freedom isn't free—
Everyone needs to serve
And hold nothing in reserve—
A love of country
Could then be understood.

A Barrack's Cell

> one wall is stared upon with sense and reason–
> it was the first wall built by the best men,
> the wall of reason is ugly, but then
> truth is not always a cut of beauty.

I'm in my room where dandelions bloom
Up into the walls of my inner thought;
In this room dwells the sanctum of a tot
And the arena just outside the womb.

This one room is the mother of my fate,
The sister and brother of irony,
The father of childish and mature hate–
This room is my entire family.

I'm in my room where forests crowd you in
Among people of all philosophy,
With their children languishing in new sin
And their dead as martyrs of honesty.

> this wall needs no particular season–
> one dimly lit wall stands for all treason.
> on the outside is the same brick wall
> conforming to architect and brick man
> and held together by a madman's season.

Between these walls where conspiracy looms
There is something makes me feel inferior,

Much less knowledgeable of coming doom
Than he who holds closed the maddening door.

This is my room where colors decorate
And synthetic objects of art exhume
The true harshness of man's longing to wait
And not accelerate life in any room.

I'm in my room shivering from the cold
From the loose window of late December
Fearing death from a love untold
And laughing at the tragedy of her.

Here inside my room, pipes speak out on terms
Conversing with me as an only son,
The unwise instrument of an interim
Age of man whose rules are the only ones.

>   the biggest wall of them all is yet small,
>   it contains the door leading to a hellish hall.
>   this wall is for patriotic thinking,
>   on one side is rebellion and an ordered hope,
>   on the other side is a heavenly rope.

And
In my room, where my bed is my only friend,
The only one I have complete trust in -
And its only fault is the window's near wind,
But a bed's advice can save one from sin;
Through sleep you can find where you've been.

I'm in my room where lights shine bright and dull
Where shadows contain all the grace that you blend,
And variable loves build a strong hull
For a ship that sails into lighter dark.

In my room, cell, cubicle—my loves fall
And are placed into the memory stall,
A rack of loves to cry about at night,
Though the memory stall's stone casts my flight.

I would like to conclude your nowhere mood,
I would like to set me free of this place–
Give me a real life, something in nature
Throw at me, fellow man, a little grace.

> then there is the wall of fantasy and farce
> the wall of posters, psychedelic whims,
> this wall stands for fun and my beer drinking
> this wall is stagnating, almost reeking,
>
> there have to be better highs if life is for living.

And in the sum of the future's end,
There grows a rose that has moss on its stem
And yet that same rose is thoughts purest, brightest gem,
Where sensitivity survives to pollinate sister fare
And their products of consciousness
Float about my room's air.

Stuff

Why'd he steal my stuff?
He's my friend,
Why'd he rob my stuff?
What's money to friends?

Why'd he steal some of my stuff?
A watch my grandmother gave me;
It's not funny to me
To be robbed by buddies,
To be hurt so senselessly,
To be placed under money .
So!
Why' d he steal my stuff?
He was a friend,
Why'd he rob my stuff?
I'm so obsessively sure
He took my stuff—

Then one day, I saw
Another one with my stuff.
My judgment had gone,
completely astray.
So… why did this other guy
Steal some of my stuff?

An Earth Burnt Black

I can't imagine
An Earth burnt black;
Yet—as I walk along in my dream—
In my mind's eye of some future regime,
I see all the grass and trees burnt black.

Nothing living only ashes cover the ground
As far as my sorrowful eyes can see
There's nothing green—even the size of a pea.
I keep walking, wondering how—
What answer could there be?

Only a nuclear war or a fire from God
Could cause the Earth's total destruction.
I can only imagine a cloud of mankind
Set free with such enormous decree
To scorch the Earth and all Humanity.

Somewhere, there is a principality,
A totally wicked, darkness of power;
Understanding and directing
Such evil to strike in only one hour—
The smoke of our ruins, a reminding tower.

Satan laughs at our deceitful defeat!
We mocked God again and again
And it will surely, most assuredly,
Come to pass that ashes and rubble
Are the only visions left of our past.

I walk along this blackened path
And I can see our future destiny.
A world that cast God aside
And let the arrogant mind of man live,
To burn the Earth to a cinder of ash-dust.

We must, at once, dust off the soles of our feet
And retreat from this less morally defined path.
There must be some way to bring evil men
To their senses and right minds....
Because—I can't imagine the Earth burnt black.

To see in a dream what is bound to be,
The dream keeps coming back to me;
Every single blade of grass burnt black.
Such an enormous tragedy of the night—
Oh, Jesus come quickly....
Save us from this ghostly sight.

Our children need a safe place to sleep at night,
A comforter to hold them tight,
Oh, Jesus come with all your might....
These elite and lustful people know you not
And seek to destroy themselves and one another
In their jealous ideology of mindless plunder:
We call to our Father to put them asunder.

Imagining

I can't imagine
What it would be like
If WW III came
With its sin entity.

I can't imagine
What slaughter there'd be
Of people free and unfree;
WW III is unworthy, surely.

I can't imagine
Why people are warrish
When love is free
And the Earth a beautiful regime.

I can't imagine
What damage we would see
If WW III came,
Even next month—early.

I can't imagine
Or truly conceive
How it could be
In God's territory!

I can't imagine
Visualizing the horrors of nuclear war.. ..
Seeking any kind of relative answer
To quantify,

Such an enormous inhumanity
Of the Devil's resounding insensitivity.

I can only visualize and imagine
The pinnacle of dark powers
Laughing at our dreadful conceit.
We must, at once,
Retreat from this mad deceit.

WW III is coming, most precariously—
Unless we can change our humanity
To a more loving kind
Of strength thru obedience—
And live to enjoy
Our Godly assurance.

Doomed

We are doomed they say...
I say, 'we're doomed not.'
This war is limited—
Here in South East Asia,
And
Not an all-out horror.

Merely to step back and take a look,
We could escape this excruciating hook.
The facts are in and we can't win;
But, then again, we can't lose
Anything but our prideful skin.
Peace comes closer by the day,
It must in today's nuclear way.

Nixon Administration

They're still trying to "keep John Lennon out,"
to keep our beautiful America stout.
the melting pot once stood for a lot…
they taught me about it in grade school,
they taught us to pray and love
and repeat the pledge of allegiance;
but they never said anything about
"keeping a guy like John Lennon out."
Many have given more, some less,
but what is the value of a John Lennon?
He took drugs—he let his body be stormed—
shunned Jesus and mocked Godly perseverance.

Yes, John Lennon may be a bad image to America.
But, I would not want to be in the shoes of the man
who is trying to "keep John Lennon out."
What can be said about this inequity—
who has the toothpick and who has the log?
Imagine such a continual disparity
of these two men of lesser humility,

these two men of intransigence ability—
fighting a war of words and intentions
in a country of a vision lost to a mere mortal destiny;
only to be saved by the undeniable eternal
sovereignty of a power of unimaginable clarity.

Our Savior comes to watch over such shortcomings and accusations and put us in a more proper place, where His mercy and compassion can lead us to heavenly grace.

JFK and LBJ

I look back and I can see
the tyranny of this time searing,
scaring all who partake or initiate.
JFK tried to reason us away from the war;
he saw the coming horror—
young men fighting and dying
senselessly in a tangled jungle war.
His words were -"In the final analysis,
it is their war to win or lose."
though some blame him for what
others would come to choose.

Talking to the generals,
LBJ said–"Get me elected and
I will give you your damn war."
Never visualizing the nightmare
in his hawkish and mindless debonair
of what the young troops would have to bear.
Stopping communism's dominos
seemed the best bet—surely we could do it,
the victory was certainly set.
There was no way to lose
yet no systematic plan of attack
for this very different topography
where tunnels and bamboo traps are at.

It would be just a limited engagement,
just a quick blow to load our resume

with another freedom quenching pose—
we didn't stop to think ahead
of how much killing and blood we might shed.
Or that China would once again
raise its ugly head and joyfully
punch us squarely in the gut
and establish a new sorrowful rut.
History began this morning and
North Korea was a mere ancient loss;
to LBJ and his friends of cavalier thoughts.

Then, came the "Gulf of Tonkin"
and such deception rolled quickly in.
Without fighting to win—LBJ is the one
who led us into this nightmare of sin.
He propped his feet up on the presidential desk,
never realizing the uselessness of his whim—
he would never back up us mostly young men,
but left us to die, over and over again,
in this mess that should never have been.

Robert McNamara and his intelligent management,
and LBJ and all the rest, so far away,
could never feel intimately the hell of this mess.
Finally, a compassion was found and delivered
by a young American people's crowd….shouting:
"LBJ, LBJ, how many kids did you kill today?"
But in the end—it was all about him—
such a staunch leader and strong within,
"pissants" were what he called many a men;
so who were we, then, after the loss of 20,000 men?

Reluctant, and with no resolve—
too scared to advance into the North,
how much was the worth of any young man?
Even one life was too much to lose
in such an unholy debacle from within
Satan's plan for the destruction of men.
LBJ left so many young men to bleed and die
in a more and more meaningless
muddy, bloody, quagmire of sin—
and the repose of such a hellish din.

No mercy or kindness did he show;
this man of somewhat questionable moral fiber.
So many scandals swept under the rug,
covered by brain matter and Kennedy's blood—
eating lunch with Hoover his close friend
and rejoicing about Oswald and Ruby's demise;
such wickedness had been very precise.

Johnson and his stately cabinet men
all met in the Oval office—over and over again—
and couldn't come up with something
they could do to stop and eliminate,
More and More names upon the wall,
More and More suffering for us all.

As the night tracers fly from our M-60 machine guns,
the AK-47 rounds often fly in and thru us—
Cong rocket propelled grenades race in
to destroy bunkers and airplanes among us—
there is no time to retrieve any happiness

and hopeless terror comes crashing upon us—
12,000 miles from home—we seem so alone.
It just seems there is no mental soundness.
And we push it aside, we set it apart....
until our guts are spilled out in a muddy ditch
and the wounded bleed all around us—

Just...
another day defending a South Vietnamese government,
serving on bases built by Brown and Root—
good friends of a sort with LBJ—
were they really in cahoots?
This self-elevated man with no real heart,
choosing personal power over our blood
as he safely counts his money in Texas hill country...
over and over and over again.

To end this war, could have been so easy,
but that thought made them queasy,
a lost election would make them so uneasy:
therefore, we had to fight and fight some more
till 58,000 plus were seen on earth no more.
Such an immoral travesty with all its horror....
and another 250,000 plus lay wounded in the dusk.

Some men did something—
to start this war—they had to kill Kennedy,
thru their power and ungodly creativity—
they hid their lies and ungodly mobility ...
Such power and delusion
that they could rule effectively;

these men, they killed Kennedy
and relaxed in their principality,
never realizing their immorality.

Still,
We want the truth, even now, even more so,
and not more lies and condensation;
redacted darkness and singularity
of selfish thought…..
herein the deep state got its start.

And indeed,
especially for those heroes who are heavenly—
let us not blindly blame John F. Kennedy.

Of Legislators and Fools

In recent years, man's fears have grown
From senseless assassinations of the well-known.
The NRA says free gun laws and no register
And the others say no guns and thus no slaughter.

In my time, it was first John F Kennedy,
A man asking what he could do for his country.
And Bobby and Martin Luther King,
What murderous madness an assassin brings.

Many men die of gun wounds each day
And there will always be guns—most will say.
Maybe the man behind the gun needs legislation,
For man is the one and only insane lethal weapon.

Assassins are a sick and neglected few
Who might well be helped by a church pew,
But where are the minds of the legislators?
Sometimes they also seem a sick and neglected few.

Making unrealistic wishes of what man should be
By controlling his weapons—is Tom foolery.
What we need is a Pastor on every street corner—
Helping us realize that this is a matter of morality.

Grieving Widows

As a widow grieves for her fallen soldier
she must contend with not only sadness
but the deviant smiles of those who carry signs
and seek to terrorize her worst time.

Her brave soldier who died out of sight...

A new widow crying tears—hoping for God's love
not the theft of her touching, poignant thoughts—
by a gang like group of devilish revelers in Satan's delight;
displaying such profane ridicule of a lonely woman's plight.

Demons from hell possess this man's unforgiving mind...

This man, his daughters and their family of hate
have so skillfully crafted our hopeless fate—
as we sit and watch and mismatch his hate;
a dismal abyss of hopelessness and despair awaits.

Oh Lord, it's just not fair...

We sit and twist about like frightened animals
as the war widow grieves to no known relief,
astonished as she is by well-wishers and friends
yet overcome so completely by this man of sin.

Oh God in Heaven, it hurts deep down thru her skin...

Another funeral, another day, another way,
they still come to deny any innocence
to the truly bereaved and instead lay claim

to all righteousness for their sinfulness.

Oh, Dear Lord, they try to judge your unimaginable,
unfathomable and unknown mysterious way…

Man's law allows and protects all this gone astray,
but God's true law is not split in two—
by this man and his sons and daughters too;
yet, our cowardice against his sin is telling true.

Oh, Lord, God Almighty, reign this man in…

Grieving widows see the death and suffering of their children;
is there nothing we can all do and try to be wise?
A fallen soldier and his family deserve respect—
to do nothing—we all become fools too.

Lawyers from Kansas they most surely are…

Interpreting sin and judgment, as only they can—
magnifying hate where there is already heartache
and smiling at the suffering grief and anguish
they present to this widow and her children—
protesting with signs and slurs,
screaming at Godly people—
they will not repent
of the devil's plan
to spread sin
all across this land.

Moreover….

God the Father sees their sin

and He will come again
and He will come in
and I would not like to be
In their den—then.

PART THREE
Personal Matters

The Fool On The Hill

My thoughts seem to be those
Of the Fool on the Hill;
With not thoughts rational have I
Chose to erect my imaginary will.

All my life has been controlled by others—
People who as often as not I've loved,
But I've seldom had my druthers
And a third of my life is smothered.

School, work, and the service,
I'm ready for my own life.
Life can be an inhuman vice
And I'm needing a wife.

I want to work at what I choose,
Not at what some computer assembles.
So it wouldn't surely surprise me
If someday I might excel assuredly.

Escaping to a freedom and set sail—
Away from the bondage of these
People of substance who desire to
Transpose me into a slave of Reluctance.

Instead I'll fly away from their pattern
And breeze above such low expectation;
Gliding upon my own theoretical clouds—
Trusting only God's will and benevolent
Dimension.

Electric Brains

Electric brains vibrate in pure harmony,
In today's polarized world of electric eccentricity.
Resisters diminuize as fibers of matter reverberate
And electric objects are generic yet always ornate.
Thoughts electric are bounced diagonally
Off and about the walls of the electric brained symphonies.
Senses too radical live in the electric dimension;
While cyber circuits ionize to concentric invariability.
Electric brains are not to be ate,
Because the transferences are villains who wait.
Mystery causes fear in an era now lovely,
Whereas fear is to be ate quite readily.

Motorcycle Clock

Don't want a wall with a plaque,
Want a motorcycle with a clock.
Don't want a mother with a gun,
Want a girl that likes my fun.

Got to make it to the dance on time,
Hear heavies sing and play their rhyme.
Don't want a wall with a plaque,
Want a motorcycle with a clock.

Like to play and romp on the lakefront,
Like to lay in the green grass with her—
Don't want a mother with a gun,
Want a girl that likes my fun.

And if she's got a motorcycle with a clock,
All we'll ever do is rock.

Cruising the Drag

Two buddies cruising the drag on this warm Chinook night…
Back and forth, up and down Main Street,
Trying to understand our place here in Great Falls:
We're looking for love from the car window up.

Speculating about what is now mostly out of sight….
Rhythmically driving up and down Main Street,
Listening to the Beatles or maybe Melanie,
First gunning it, then slowing down to find cute babes.

A beautiful young lady at the next street light,
With long hair flowing—such an intriguing sight,
"Will you ladies meet us at Tracy's Cafe for a quick bite?"
Our young and naive energy is exploding this summer night.

We wait but they don't come, so we talk of past romances,
Hoping love to shower down sensuous hail upon us,
Our dreams turn to heavenly situations and womanly fragrances;
Burnt rubber and exhaust—please, oh please, flee from us.

A full Moon is enticing us and we're back on Main Street
With its train station parking lot and turning point on the North end
And Texas Tom's drive thru—the return slot to head North once again;
Surely this night will never end, but the base is beckoning tomorrow's spin.

Finally,
We're just two Airmen sitting on the bus stop bench
At Eleventh Street or on the Super Sport's hood,
Which is glowing warm from the 396 engine beneath,
Wrung out by the four-speed, quadra jet and posi rear end.

Expecting love to come, happens to all not some—
Gibson Park to the east is where all is said and done.
After you find a girl—no need to cruise anymore—
Just park and talk of dreams and delights.

A girlfriend would make it all fit together,
Solving the mystery of so many searching nights.
No more need to race down the street and just look cool,
Just a forward looking desire to tie a knot of love forever.

Meanwhile....
We watch all the young ladies drive by and some wave,
Eventually we will meet our supple matches,
At some future and seemingly fate planted time—
But tonight, our charm has gone so sadly unclaimed.

We wish we were as powerful as this machine of muscle,
Wishing we could find a couple of young ladies
To have a friendly tussle, but this night is now gone....
Our quest will have to take a rest, Main Street wins once again.

Headed South to the base, hurriedly, a chirp from second gear,
Three thousand, four thousand revs throw us back—
Tonight this Super Sport Chevy is our best friend,
Giving us, if somewhat reluctantly, a reason to grin.

A Subconscious Mind

Only your subconscious mind
knows what truth there lies
within the memory cells of your mind.
In comparison, my other mind cries,
subconscious and automatic it is—
the hidden mind flashes through
the misguided human mind's view
and it really does benefit you.
For you see, it's true
you have but one real mind
deep inside the brain of you.
Dreams are often too real
and should not be left behind,
forever congested in your hidden mind.

Used

I feel as if used…
I mean, as in daily life
To play a chosen role
As cast by someone else.

It worries me sometimes so
To know, I'm programmed
To perform the show
As it surely must go.

A calling from above
Does it come like a Dove?
Or super naturally—
No details do I know.

Such a mystery
Comes not easily,
I need to act
Oh so expediently.

A blessing from God
And I've acted so feebly
But my master knows
My heart speaks truthfully.

My work will come
At His time frame.
I cannot fail this trial
Or act against all Godly wisdom—
Given me.

I feel used, you see—
Life's mine but I'm not free.
People need me, evidently—
My joy returns upon request
Yes, Lord, I'll do my best.

Though everyone has a talent
Godly and inspiringly;
To work and sail
The sea of Spirituality.

So used, I guess, I'll gladly be,
A tool as He needs me....
Not as I see me,
But as He wills me.

Special Effects

Girl, you do things to me
That no other girl has,
You cause special effects
In my body and mind.
Never before have I had
The urge to destruct,
But if a strange boy selects
To look at you, a nerve goes nuts
And only with brotherly luck
Will he escape my strong looks of reject.

Girl, you cause special effects
In my body and mind.
I've never been so jealous
But the thought
Of someone taking you away
Makes my emotions rebellious.

And when we settle down to kiss,
A special effect of bliss
You do cause me to feel….
You're something I don't want to miss.

And when I have a problem or two—
I just dream of you
And my elation solves them.
Your thoughts are so pure to me.

Your special effects are groovy
And I hope that I accordingly
Cause some special effects in you.
For that is Love's sweet gravity
And a wonderful compatibility.

Saying Goodbye

I love them all very much
And I never even knew it,
You really see love
When it comes time to leave.

I love them— all very much
And to leave is to die inside,
Luckily, men don't cry
But still, they must say goodbye.

I love them—all very much
Yet yesterday, I didn't know;
I thought only of them as friends
And now they sigh, cry, and some say why.

It's only for a year—
But my Mother is crying at the door
And Dad is proud inside but feeling fear
And me, I really don't wanna leave here.

I love them— all very much
And it's better actually;
For when I return, you'll see,
A more compassionate me
And how I'll love them
All so very much more.

Families

Love makes the world go around
And love is a product of family life—
A family is a group of related people
Who live together and form one complete love thought.

There are so many families in the world—
Though, there are just as many un-families,
These, being, the very lonely lost people
And other unfortunates of life's declared purpose
Who live happily or unhappily and trapped
As similar and yet as opposite
Of what was meant to be.

The un-families know no love or emotional bonds,
Yet, it is a crime for these people to be not of one
Complete love thought— but do they really care?
The father or mother is not really there;
Choosing to locate their children
In some kind of outer despair.

A family is needed by all to be happy.
A family that can cure everlasting loneliness,
Is a blessing so secure and so sure.
Bit by bit the family unit is built,
A monument to fit God's plan—
One man and one woman
Who will take a heavenly stand.

TALK

I enjoy talking to her—
She talks cute with a slight slur.
Our talks are long
And so prolific—
We talk along terrific.

I enjoy talking to her—
Her accents are so emotional
And her humor, not puritanical.
Her stories are so imaginable;
Seems like I'm really there... .
Her expressions most contortioned
And her replies lovingly understandable.

I enjoy talking to her—
Her voice is soft
And represents quite a lot;
Depicting memories caught
By the voice our love has sought.

Life Size

The tinseled roof of time
reflecting all that is mine,
casts my seduction aside,
and remains to hide
the tinseled wall of time.
Your memories and mine,
seeking pleasures so fine;
making me an inhabitant
walking through this dark night.
Knowing not what I might
see in eternity's real delight;
a more depictive realistic time
where everything is presently bound
in a Love from our creator's storehouse
that is ever so easily found.
Somewhere we know it lies,
real time, and not of Our eyes,
beside all the deception, the lies
real memories, un-tinseled….life size.

Gotta Be Near You All of the Time

Gotta be near you all of the time.
I'm selfish—but because
My love is strong,
Gotta be near you all of the time.
But only if you'll give your love,
all of your love—
not a portion, but everything
to me, today, then I've
Gotta be near you all of the time.
What else is there for all time?
To consummate…
what is yours and mine
please say to me that—
You've
Gotta be with me all of the time.

Of Bushes and Bees

She was a rose bush and myself a bee.
I came and I watched in a nearby tree....
At first by accident and then from intrigue,
At the beginning so easy to leave;
But fall and love came and me the bee stayed—
More often hidden while big plans were laid.

Time was growing short and love maturing
For me the bee—so domineering.
But what right of a bee to approach a rose bush?
Though sent from heaven a bee and a bush
Are not forgiven to only one love...
Though that would be real grace from above.

Bees and bushes do have their attractions—
But so many bees hide in un-esteemed sanction.
To become free and not a vehicle of no traction
Might be a blessing—full of Godly action.
To decipher your love and bring it full
Upon the imagined love—and you'll know why—
It beats shyness and inaction!

Your Breeze

There is no breeze for me to glide—
no path set for me to follow,
only memories of your love
as my mind drifts to fields of you.
So feminine, so tender, so frilly…
where everything is a plenty,
where fruit trees bear golden honey
and our day lives everyday sunny
as though heaven sent us to be.
I miss the twinkle of your eyes,
the curly flowing of your long blonde hair
and how our hearts molded together—
The not forgotten mystery of your way
nor the gentle caress we both divined,
for ours was a love always entwined.
Now, the night goes and goes, the torture grows.
Sulking in my pool of no reflection
I cast my fate all prayer relation,
and lovingly long for you—

Knowing I so need the sweet savory scent
of your one and only breeze
from half way around the world,
so far for a breeze to flow.....

Green Grass

Green grass is so heavenly
And sometimes such a good remedy
For you and me and our far away hearts;
Without green grass, we'd be but dissembled parts.

Thank God for nature's grass seas
Which can set our minds at ease,
On sunlit days—green meadows for wild bees;
Green days were made for you and me.

The grassy beauty calms our loneliness
And brings us closer with love's hope
That soon we might walk together
On a soft green slope.

Green days were made for you and me,
A blanket, sunlight and shade…
The essence of your touching care;
The soft green grass is memory's flair.

Silent Atmosphere

Sitting in my silent atmosphere
crying out to the Comforter in my sphere.
Knowing that I treated you so badly,
I count the minutes of my sadness—
and wake, for sleep brought me here.

Gazing into your atmosphere
wondering if part of you is still here,
with me, despite my ignorant calamity.
I see your face cast with my love's hate.
A dream I hope or only a fear?
Will I get another chance to persevere?
To make things right about that night,
to beg like a dog for forgiveness again,
knowing how wrong I've been.

Re-thinking the way of my atmosphere;
of all the trodden morals and broken mirrors,
of my place so distant from you—
filled with war and death and time
and mostly just the wild atmosphere
of my mind.

Expecting Love

Expecting love to come
Happens to all, not some.
It's almost the best part
Of love and its heart;
Waiting for love at first sight
To blossom into full moon light
And the savor of flowers sweet,
Not to mention heaven's feat.
The mystery of the sum is there:
Among the forest of the sea,
About the rivers of casting doubt,
Never predicting the outcome of the joust.
Then it will happen in all its force—
True happiness arrives not short—
Expecting love to come
Happens to all, not some.
It's in our hearts
Such a positive
Thing to say.

Treat You Right

He can treat you right and I can't,
He can take you places all right
And he can treat you to what I can't,
But I'll be happy without you tonight.

I loved you at first sight
And gave all the love of me,
But his money brings light
Upon your heart transparency.

He can buy you glamour and fun
Another day with him in the Sun;
A boat, a sports car, and fancy clothes
And he can give you anything.

I'll keep looking—I'm not done,
I just thought you were the one.
So many nights working together,
Sharing thoughts and funny humor.

You gave me my best moments
In a lonely time of my reflection
And now he has made it—
All come undone.

One

I always thought I knew her so well—
Then she stole all the love my mind had stored,
All the memories a love cell could hold,
My happiness with life's love had been sold.

And though I hate myself so
And can't let her memory go,
It's something time should have cured,
Only tomorrow will tell for sure.

Now I retreat to my forest of past
Promising myself a secure love fast –
A love of no possible faults or flaws,
A love to withstand the most human claws.

All the while....
Still replaying thoughts, sights and sounds
Of the previous love gone out of bounds;
So sweet, so pure, how can I get back to her.

21 December 1969

You're the last girl that will put me down,
Never again will I volunteer to be a clown,
Never shall I give my love first—
Don't want my love dispersed.

So you put me down
And run around
But look what I've found—
The answer to you
And my feeling blue.

He may have a car:
A bright red Corvette
And a sleek ski boat for two,
Snazzy leather shoes
And did I mention,
A letterman's coat too?

His money is unending—
But I must have something too,
Though it escapes me to explain
How I could possibly compete
With this package of dynamically
Assembled man about town.

I guess my chances just stink
And I'm left with my 59 Chevy,
With an empty tank and big fins

And only a dollar or two
But my heart is all into you…

There's not much I wouldn't do
For another chance to sway you,
To me you're the biggest catch,
Much bigger than a Corvette
Or a Ski Nautique or silver too.

I just want to hold you so tight
Till all the other guys are out of sight;
Come ride with me in my old Impala
For a romance that's true.

Far Away

Could have had a girl tonight,
could have gone downtown alright
but you mean more than that—
your love is my mood's only track.
Might have dreamed bad things all night
and though your feel is so far away;
I know our love knows only one way.
The others do alright by me
for I am not the judge of one, two, or three—
their will is so their own and maybe free—
until later—when it turns into calamity.
And so a journey will not be mine tonight,
I'll stay here and stay awake and alone
knowing, hoping someday I'll be home
though even now, I can feel you near
ever so far away, my dear.

By The Day

he writes the letter by the day
to his wife so far away
speaking of the war's proximity,
the very closeness of hell's way.
a show at the base theater
even makes his letter sound neater.
then tonight he'll sneak away
to a maiden through the darkness
beating thoughts of fear arrear,
smoking pot so he can think clear,
no thoughts of shame entering here ?
Yet,
Still embracing the thought of his far-off wife,
their years together—their children too
and, I guess, wishing she were true too!

After Three Children

John left Sue for Joan after three children
And the doctor's wife is taking all kinds of pills.
A soap opera here,
Some drama there—
Sensationalism and adrenalin
Often make for unaccounted life bills.
It's hardly ever fun
Or un-aggravating
But people defy some
And find devastating
Happiness or love—
The ever most fun.
And to be sad really makes some people glad,
So used to sorrow that self pity isn't bad…

One Outlook

It's a bachelor's night off—
He is thinking thoughts soft,
About women who might be on the make
And wondering which one he will tonight take.
A son he always wanted
Will be a dream forever hunted.
To enjoy pleasure is his single issue
And numerous loves his visions pursue.
To him there is no loving consistency,
Only many moments spent on a lonely sea—
Which will fill his life
With consequence and unfortunate transparency—
In this land of the speakeasy night…
And scatter away what really delights—
A woman waiting back home
In her loving true and kind hope
That he might hold her thought tight
Throughout this and every overseas night,
One more and one more, far away night….

PART FOUR
Spiritual

Prehistoric

Man is a primate who wanders slowly
On towards a lighter dark and days of young.
A being of so little objectiveness
Put forth to be loved of someone other—
Until maturity and sense are born
Into all thought of he who walks the earth.

What moral virtue can be said of man at this stage?
His history is no true love of you—
Belittlement, wars, love and always the death:
What does man see in the stars and the moon?
And most important, who or what lies controlling
His ever and ever more prideful thoughts?

To revere the properties of life itself,
We must admit the undeniable truth:
That our life began in our Father's heaven
And not in some cosmic and organic pond,
Or in someone's vain imaginations
Of scientific prose and convenient clatter;
Unborn lives are important and not a laughing matter.

Though now some come to reverse this matter
And justify away mere baby circumstance,
Enabling millions and millions
To die the babies' death of defenselessness;
Unable to hide or fight valiantly back
Is such a losing predicament.

Yet,
For everyone at Tea—living the life of Luxury,
This seems like social justice
To be able brush off such inconvenience,
As the hard hearted continue this sea of blood
Which will surely burn them through
When all is said and done.

I pray a path is set for man of earth,
A light that will come and shine
And illuminate the truth, for then,
We could give full importance to birth!

Heaven and Hell

Why people fight
Is beyond my sight
When all the time happy
They really might be.
Yet, they'll argue and even kill,
I just don't know
But earth could be Hell.
The god of this world
Has been zeroing in
With his demons and sin
To kill, steal and destroy
Any inch we will give him.
When it's time to measure my sin—
I'll say to Him above—
And not to him below—
"I'm ready for Heaven,
In Hell I've already been."

This Thing Called Time

Time destroys more love than a war destroys men.
Time away from one's love makes one wonder of when....

Time, you scoundrel, look what you've done to me.
See where you left my soul to be:
feel all the hurt you've done to me,
touch the melancholy of my being,
hear my cries of anguish seething,
listen to mutterings of a hopeful future,
taste the malnutrition of a lost love,
and devour that love in moments not hours—
Endlessly counting through a slow year.

Envision the decaying crevices
of the floor of a once strong love
and inhale the premeditated conspiracy
of the attitude of the human dynasty....
To fight you, Time, to reclaim
all that you take from this boy
is the destiny of all earthlings come since.

Time, you can be a villain and nothing else—
In Time there lies the answer to oneself.

In Heaven no one knows of Time,
only the present existence
of Joy and Fulfillment—for GOD
has taken our worldly fears
and cast them far away.

Chaffing of Beauty

Fire and ice, blindly fulfilling,
we dashed a run so revealing;
peace for us—a chaffing of beauty—
bounding through the night before.
As newlyweds on our special shore—
we consummated a communion
of a long wait away from this moonlit shore.
Now we felt our bodies so tightly bound together;
one joyous body formed and joined forever.
Surely this is heaven to be found—
to fight for till the end of time
when she let hers be mine…

Day and Night

What right has the night to linger on so?
Who told anyone that the day was right?
Only dusk and dawn satisfy urges
And create surges of talent outright.
So, people of now make use of each dawn
And ignore not the setting Sun,
For these are the times
That give light to dark—
That annihilates delays of fright,
That delineates wrong from right.
With these last days upon us—
Give voice where silence lingers.
One comes to steal, kill and destroy—
And another waits patiently and anticipates,
Watching over us and absorbing
Our acts of and toward salvation—
Our compassionate free will and obedience,
And Godly motivations found within and without.
The Son of Man will come and save us
From the devil's slithering darkness
As we contemplate eternity's radiance.

Fog

The fog is a friend.
It seeps, creeps and about you bends,
Trying so hard to conceal
All that is normally revealed.

Fog saunters slowly,
Such an imagination has the fog
And can be seen as hellish or holy—
The main element of our lingering uncertainty.

The fog is also a most ghastly foe…
To great lengths it can send
Normal surroundings to hellish bins—
The fog resembles the Devil's den.

But then again, there are mighty angels too,
Who can shine right through
Where the Devil has been
And eliminate all traces
Of the lies, the deceptions,
And such fogged over
And hidden misconceptions.

The Retarded Children's Ward

You should have seen,
Some of those children
At the Kansas State
Retarded Children's Ward.
Many were deformed
And helpless and
I wanted to cry
Long and hard
And so profusely....

In the Kansas State
Retarded Children's Ward;
Where Porky Pig and Donald Duck
Covered the walls—
To entertain these young ones.
But there was no joy found here,
It had long since vanished
With the burden the nurses carried;
Amidst the shrieking howls of these children
Who only wanted to be normal
And now locked away
In these sterile white walls.

I only came for a day
But I've never forgotten
The sights of that short stay.
Now, to be thankful every day
And pray for God's healing

To those locked away and alone.
They will never know the freedom
That we take for granted everyday:
A walk through a sunlit park,
A baseball game, under lights, after dark,
The blessing of loving their own children,
Or becoming one flesh with another.
Maybe there is a purpose to everything,
To find our humility when none is known.
My tears I've cried for those young souls
In the Kansas State Retarded Children's Ward..

At 21

Learned a lot being here all caught,
learned a lot about life and rot,
know now that I'm no longer a tot,
around me there's a universal uniqueness—
not a personality seeking meekness.
People being people true, brewing you,

not knowing who will suffer their dreams delight.
Before I was a child wondering in a foggy night—
wondering and pondering to myself,
which one is the Devil and which one is right?
There are endless valleys of sensual night alleys,
pleasures so full of emotional delight—

bottomless canyons of passion and plight,
trinkets of thrill to lead one from sight.
A most colorful rainbow of feeling with no pot to lure,
no reason for anyone to be completely sure,
a waterfall cascades over my thoughts;
the water is bright, clean and clear—

my thoughts have resumed to be pure
and walk on the way of the narrow path
avoiding these Devilish lures....

A Mutual Thing

God came through for me,
I can't say why—you see
But when I ask, I do receive
Not always in full, but to help me.
My God does love me,
He must, or why else would I be?
It's a mutual thing
For on some days God asks
And I try to help
Him receive.

Behind the Back Talk

"Behind the back talk" is commonary
To all people of the human natuary;
For it's enjoyable to gossip pleasantly
About someone's shortcomings, most secretly.

It wouldn't be said to the face,
Or in the exact face, t'would be fun's waste .
It's got to be spoken in unkindly taste
Behind the poor person's space.

And the victim can't even defend
Or retaliate against the remarks
That are being said against his character;
"Behind the back talk" is not evolutionary.

The Preacher

The young preacher man
talks of life and God
and finding happiness in
the world around you.
He preaches brotherly love
and moral responsibility and
heaven above, but then he is
only a young preacher man.

The middle-aged preacher man
tells of his fears of the wicked world;
how man is failing his God
and how the Holy Spirit works.
He is not happy or sad—
but neither is his God;
to completely rely on flowing sand
is the purpose of this preacher man.

The older preacher man
is an embellished voice machine.
He proclaims— repent and most fully
believe in Christ's humble and holy divinity.
He shouts for us to look above
for a Dove coming through the clouds;
and his church is surely built on rock
and not upon some non-believer's thought.

Forty Below

It was forty below
And only five did show
For the 9 o'clock Protestant services—
So, we had a discussion of many discourses.
Not unlike a businessman's meeting
Or a stockholder's annual briefing—
We talked of love of God
In objective and subjective nods
And about the grace of God
And about the set standards
For reaching a heavenly destiny.
To be specific, they had it in the bag,
Such heavenly thoughts spirited them on.
Listening to the quotes
Of a preacher's wife of Methodist ways,
The taught thoughts of a young religious couple
And answering questions religiously supple:
The Pastor knew all the details we had missed;
All the better paths we had not taken.
Trivia and detail of argumental wails—
They quoted the Bible and I (had only) life....
My life of mostly self-righteous strife.
I was outnumbered, badly so and broken,
My skimpy knowledge shaken
By these people of more devoted ways
Who had feared God all their days.
Their stockholders meeting

Now made sense to a repentant me;
They had taken stock in things Godly
And I had taken stock in only me.
Not a business meeting as I had pretended;
They displayed knowledge and love
That was unknown previously to me.
As His chosen children,
They were so kind to me—
What I really needed
Was to be taken over someone's knee—
Like an errant child pleading relentlessly
For a selfish win over another…
I now realized there was more
Respect that was becoming of me.

We prayed and left church—
With the bitter wind chill
Smacking me in the face, too.
And at ten o'clock, I had been humbled,
And thankfully so, but…
In Great Falls, Montana
It was still forty below.

The Service Church Situation 1968

It is a church paid for by the government,
It is a church for men in the armed services
Assigned graciously and stamped approvingly,
With a US government—please don't offend anyone—
Government endorsed faithful preacher man.

Given the oath and pledged undying faith
To God, servicemen and the US government,
Primarily and mostly just like the rest of us.
And they come, the people who attend this holy abode;
Mostly spouses, dependents and any other ones stationed here,
This church was built for these worthy people of service.

Constructed by servicemen, for servicemen
And operated solely by various servicemen.
But,
As I attend this church I am saddened,
Although I believe it is a church's purpose to gladden.
There is this Viet Nam war going on about—
Killing, murdering, and slaying many men stout,
But where is the prayer to end this war?
No, nobody seems to realize what a church is for;
Someone must stand and pray away the war.

A military church of patriotic ways for so many days,
We come to worship and to ask for a peaceful end,
A salvation of sorts for all of our cohorts—

We believe in God—to this most all will agree, don't we?
Or is this some kind of post Jesus decree?

Let's ask for peace in VietNam openly,
From God our true master who is listening;
Even on this day of bloody battlefield fighting,
Airmen, foot soldiers, sailors and marines too—
Are sacrificing lives for the Red, White and Blue.

Instead of letting so many church services go pending—
Without one prayer for a peace unrelenting—
We should bow our knee and pray
Our true wish of preserving all life heaven sent.
Yet, these church walls are waiting for our emotions
And not some unspoken manner of scheming

And not some politically-correct rhetoric.
The devil knows well when his plan takes hold
Against the most evident way of non-repenting.
Our men, our brothers, our brethren are dying
This very day on that battlefield so far away;
Let's not forget them and let us pray—
For God is listening to cries for help
Where the bullets fly thru the night—
As we stand here in what should be light….

Off the Wall

I am the picture,
I hang on the wall....
Sometimes tall and sometimes small.
At times in correct place
And again, often not,
For perfection is mostly just sought
And rarely found in time's haste.

I am the picture
Hanging on the wall
And little do I work at my call.
I'm nature and also abstract case,
Even smeared paste and always bought.
To some I seem an interesting lot,
But mostly my time is spent in waste—
I'm merely a reminder of nature's grace,
Or a pretty and loving face...
The redemption is in me
For the human family.
I am the picture Let me hang.

PART FIVE
Nature's Beauty

Fall

Autumn is fall
And the leaves do,
For the children
It's a hobby new.

There is football
And rain and snow
And beauty for all
As the fall months glow.

Fall is too short
And shouldn't be hurried;
Brilliant trees work
So hard to please all.

Not only grandeur is ours
But varying splendor ….
To once match the stars,
Yes, it is exquisitely tender,
Fall is a great surrender!

With the sweet savor and aroma
Of burning leaves
Can be found God's preeminence;
Of a creator
Who loves us with so much magnificence.

Lake Shawnee

I have no Grecian Urn
That needs immortalizing—
And a lake of nature
Has already outlived
The oldest man's demoralizing,
Many, many times over.

The lake is cool and quiet,
It functions swiftly and slowly;
Next to the lake
One human being seems so lonely
And reliant to He who makes.

I come and I bake
In the Sun, on the lakefront
With my petty thoughts;
Which go immediately
Exaggerated as metropolic
Theories of little ridicule,
Or forgotten as miniscule
And inexcusable un-attuned
Respites of the bright…

The lake is sunny and alive,
It has it's set mood
And a person can't brood
If the lake doesn't fully approve.

The lake has every color,
Yet, sometimes only one,
Depending upon the season
And what your mind will see.
Somewhere here, in the warm green banks,
Among the purist mist of nature's identity
Lies what must be a hidden sea
Explaining the very mystery;
Of why He wants to change
Our sadness into gladness—
Through this lake,
Lake Shawnee.

I am the Lake

I am the lake,
Come enjoy me.
There are swing sets
And pontoon boats,
Picnic tables
And many trees.

So many ultra-green meadows
With high healthy grass....
And a severing creek,
A capillary feeding the lake.
Flocks of ducks and geese
Mingling around, gliding down—

On Sundays and Holidays
And weekends too,
People come to the lake
For their nature's sake.

I am the lake—
I entertain all,
At any convenient time
Come and enjoy me.

A Horse

Saw the horse running wild,
free to conquer the countryside,
at ease to be free with all the trees—
never caring what anyone will see.

Not doubting this freedom of his—
felt the horse running wild,
parallel to the beautiful stream,
alongside his green grass mistress ....
feeling high and untethered to even thee.

When do we come to such liberty?
to run free with the trees
and enjoy God's creativity—
There is only one answer in every one of us:
To bow our knee and live humbly.

Trees Do

A girl told me she wonders why I don't smoke;
Well, to me it's just a joke.
A man offers some to me
And I say, "I don't need it to see."
My friends are curious about me
And I look for a tree…

And say, "Gee tree, do you use it too?"
Though most will digress or say no
To someone, like me.

The trees do smoke
And are members of the "in crowd"
Condoning irregularity of purpose
From within such a sin.
At least trees don't have brain cells
To burn and to lose readily
And as easily as we do.

The truth of enlightenment
Is here for everyone to see,
Anyone who has known a tree
Can understand such perplexity

For their brain's eternity…

Empty Beer Can

An empty beer can is seen:
Lying in the gutter,
Broken in the grass,
Upright in the hall,
In the bathroom stall,
Shattered against a wall,
Next to a rock at a fisherman's spot,
Still cool right during the fun,
Or glowing hot in the morning Sun.

As a sight completely uptight
An empty beer can is seen
During the era of reality lean,
Empty beer cans are the evidence
Of today's contracting human sense.

One can stands for daily gossip,
Two will often mean the start of nonsense
And three cans might mean fits of sorrow,
Though, four cans surely stand for a loneliness
Which will last into tomorrow.

And if you see an empty case,
Devote very little time
Trying to locate the vociferous waste
Of those who chose the quantity of haste—
Over a more thoughtful pace.

Some will always think with thoughts disdain,
About the people whom beer cans drain,
According to what experiences are contained
By ideals of the manufacturers of life being detained.

But what does a beer can say?
"Throw me in the gutter—
Heave me in the grass—
Sit me in a corner—"
Most surely not, not today.

Empty beer cans merely show
The meaninglessness of today's ways,
Or the meaning of un-mown grass,
For it is the grass that must come
And cover all our pukey, smelly mess.

Hey Flying Saucer

Hey flying saucer up in the sky,
How is it where you live your lies?
Do you have a God or a Guru?
Do you guys have mother-in-laws too?

Okay, flying saucer, don't answer me
And if I were you, I'd stay up where I could see,
Five o'clock traffic and smog above the trees,
Or our mini-skirted women in near striptease.

Spy, flying saucer, spy—
Fly way up high in the blue sky—
Take notes of everything below
But leave me alone, please just go.

Polluted People Prosper

Rockets to the moon,
Trash to the sky,
In the naysayer mind's eye—
We're going fast from dust to dust.

Beauty for all to see?
Products of waste, subconscious fate,
And the mountains by Saints
To overlook manly tastes.

Rusted car bodies,
DDT to control pests,
Chemicals to control rivers,
And trash to float the ocean dry.

The beauty for all to see
Could be overshadowed, you see,
By a diseased tree, saved only
By rockets to the moon.

The Machine

See the bright, pretty, new machine;
It operates very well and is super clean—
This machine is the family's joy.
It has remarkable devices to employ
And all the time it's quite coy.
See the very rich, happy merchant smile.
He has done exceedingly, upper class well.
And built up quite a money pile
With his sixty-five per cent mark up sale,
Plus taxes, plus interest, plus insurance,
Minus a trivial overhead—
Oh, what assurance!

See the family and their not-so-new machine.
The machine needs repair and isn't so clean
And the warranty won't cover the needed repair;
Such a family, sitting, grieving in utter despair.

Yet, the merchant is moving to a bigger store,
As the family treads to the house of the poor.
The merchants are ever expanding;
Globally they've developed quite a standing,
Never to be stopped or even slowed
The mother's birth of another monopoly—
A monstrosity of a socialistic ideology;
Deriving itself away from free marketry, And—
Forcing us into a so-called machine slavery.

These plans come from not just one man,
But from the powers of the air—that refuse
To exempt us from becoming less tedious
And keeping us all equally in this ditch
Of the less wealthy and non-meticulous.

PART SIX
Miscellaneous Musings

My Disobedience

Really want to go away from here…
the loneliness is building into a mad fear,
there is nothing here for me.
See the Sun rise again,
maybe it will never reach me
but leave me to lie in sin.
I walk the same street today
wishing for some different tree;
another scene from elsewhere
to squelch all relative jeers.
Going to pause in the monsoon rain,
and look for a friendly cloud—
one to understand, identify me….
not to smile clowns on me,
to love what can be left
of one left with little love.
Somehow I seem to be alone
to die the death of disobedience,
the one who listened with no sense.

Lites

The red lights are green,
the green red,
where will we be
when we're dead?

I love the memories of us,
of the rivers we swam,
the stars we glided,
the people we loved.

Thrusting memories to the front,
your thoughts sift through to me....
containing caresses too good to be true,
easing time's sting of pain, and hurt.

Loving you is all I want....

Inner Light

Thought I knew myself,
thought I saw my own inner light,
then it came to me one day—
all the shock life could bring,
all the disappointment a war could sing.
Shining through was my true inner light
diminishing what I thought me to be.
Seeing through my lonely reality
and cast so far away from home—
I was now a new day clone,
dimly lit and so alone.

Now the draft notice had come
and I stayed alone and apart;
thinking this might be the end of me,
boxed in now and not quite right…
no longer separated from fear,
because now the war came near.
Previously thinking with myself
that I might be a bright light
but at this moment,
I became;
more alone and full of fright.

Don't Care

Some people don't like me,
I don't care— that's fair.
My eyes have no mind,
my mind no eyes.
They laugh— so what
I'll never care.
Rain drops set the scene
for mean people's gleam—
in the darkest night alley,
in one of my green valleys
they stare…. they're always there.
People look don't wanna see,
the things that bother me—
why should anyone stare?
I can't help how God made me
I didn't do anything mean—
I don't care about their stares
or their vain negativity,
it's nothing to me….

Defiantly

If you could see
the reverse side of me
it speaks so defiantly,
saying: "you don't own me!"
I'm not some kind of tree,
I'm bought, paid for and a believer—
who can think free
and now I can see
how it was meant to be
of someone other than you.
Too bad—
You'll never see,
The reverse side of me.

I Ride the Wave

I ride the wave,
I surf my way
Doing my best for satisfaction
Not knowing for why.
Wiping out is easy,
It's always easier to run
Than to face the shore's far sun.
But I will stay with this thing
Until I hit the shore's end
Or am thrown helplessly
Into a humiliating defeat—
By some maturing wind.
Still,
I ride the wave,
Loving its place
And though it is a hard job
It is something I can't leave
No matter how hard I try,
It's the wave for me.

20

I sit here and I stare
And say where
Am I at?
I've been here before
Outside this door,
Alone and cold—
And I wonder why
There's no one but me
Outside this society
Of the here and now.
Who are these people
who take me away
from all I know
And what I have to say?

Don't, do not—
transport me away from here
from all that I hold dear;
what is the meaning
of these people who sear
discontent and control
into my mind's sphere

Wait

So you ask me to wait—
to hesitate,
too bad
losing you has made me sad.
Don't ask true love to wait
for it can cause a change of fate,
maybe even some silent secretive spite.
Please view the other side of things
and filter in some faith
so we don't have to wait.

My Mother Said….

My mother said:
"Son, live for today—
It's today that counts."
This is what my mother said.

She must be right—
For in today I am happy
And its tomorrow that saddens me,
Yes, my mother is very bright.

They and the merchants say:
"Look to the future."
But I would rather not
Listen to their fictitious ways.

Today always lives in yesterday
But today not always lives in tomorrow,
My mother and her heart
Are justified by history.

Haircut

Piggy's hair was very long and tangled
Due to his state of geographical isolation.
Penrod's hair was long also
Until the summer months fadation.
But since Ring's haircut—
Hair has established a new era.
An era where the older generation
Dictate hair length sensation
Or, try to.

Huck and Tom never had to worry
Of a shortened haircut's degradation;
My time has caused a young deflation.
Samson could've used more hair
After the theft of his sleepy locks,
Under empowering his final destination
Beneath the rocks.
No more can they say nay—

For the time to dictate hair length
Has come and gone.
Now hair is just long and short
And any shape or style,
Anything to make one smile.

PART SEVEN
People & Characters

Sara Beth

Sara Elizabeth
Was my grandmother
As many people have.
But she was special
And she was different
For I loved her
As I still daily do.
When I was but three
I sat upon her older knee
And was comforted by her
Oh, so graciously….
Sara Beth was the mother of mothers
To me at three.
One day, as I missed my mother,
temporarily,
She gave me cookies and milk, calming me.
She took me to church
And made me sit quietly….
In the sanctuary of our creator
Where I would return
Many years later—
Saving me from total disaster
And the Devil's plan for me—
A sweet grandmother for ever after.

John Wayne

John Wayne rides again
And the cowpoke's cowboy fights on
Through many an immortal moon;
Singing tunes to the lady folk,
Swinging fists at bad cowpokes,
And mostly winning at his thing.
It's in his face, the good guy gleam,
Being the Duke is no easy thing—
True legend to thrill all on the silver screen.

W. C. Fields

W.C. Fields is my hero,
He's one I love,
A man to be misunderstood.
Operating under some kind of
Reverse synthetic mood—
He enlightens us to a
Most nonsensical property
Of our mental insecurity
He fumbles around—
Never arriving
At any destiny....
And just deadpans
His way to hilarity.

Mother Goose

Mother Goose tells lies.
She never said
It'd be this way;
Mother Goose
Didn't explain hate
Or Shakespeare's Kate.
Mother Goose
Is a reality
Not a fantasy
But soon may become
A fatality.
For people are dehumanizing
Their characters of less perfection
And looking for
No subjection.
Mother Goose
You are not truth
Nor beauty,
And why should we
Believe in your fairy tale
When we can see
The head of the nail
And all your blurry obscurity?

The One Armed Man of Alleyways Where

The one armed man of alleyways where:
walks past eyes that do not see,
kicks a beer can against thoughts
of loneliness, of wondering despair.

He's the one armed man of alleyways where:
he would rather talk with the dogs
and flick ashes not at cat tails
and follow the run of alleyways nowhere.

The one armed man of alleyways where:
sees sadness bouncing about the muddy paths,
lingers long enough to cause a tear
then confusion and finally a mad fear.

The one armed man of alleyways where:
he has two arms in another reality
an alternate to his negative severity
and an imagined tranquility.
Rubble, scum, ashes, trash and disease
overshadow the under-shadowed troubles,
love crushes, ambition and people fear.
These, they watch menacingly
the one armed man of alleyways where…

The Reporter

I was sitting in the newsroom and feeling most alone,
Just a poor reporter who was far away from home....
When up jumps an editor with assignment in hand,
"I want this story done fast; twill be seen all over the land."

So quickly I dug into my brain for a pocketful of words
And found that in this respect I was also forlorn.
Oh panic! A story is needed and I have none borne,
Why me? Why not a tinker, a baker, or a candlestick maker?

Only forty minutes left to terminate this story
And end all my misery; is it a possibility?
Only he knows, who manages our respectability
And if I fail once more as in the past, oh woe is me.

The editor lurks very near in all his villainy—
Thus, if I fail, I will not die in humility.
But hark! I have the story done in time—
A good reporter am I; the world of news is still mine.

Apollo Eight

A lover's tool of song;
It's been there all along,
Riding high in the sky—
And now three men fly by,
Floating above and around
The mirrored, cratered rock haven.

The call of the moon
Is no small swoon—
The men are brave and adventurous.

And their thing of motivation: complextuous.
But what is more complex than man's nature?
Only the Creator of each and every molecule
Of space and time in our own visible vestibule.

Such a folly to critique the potter,
Trying to guess the theories of outer space....
Even if they properly conjure completely
God's relevance of a surety,
Man is adventuring in his maturity—
I hope to end all his vain futility.

Of Feeling Low

Negative vibes can multiply quickly,
At times, making you feel low and sickly.
For one reason or another
Your emotions will drop to a climatic low
And your thoughts will be depressingly cluttered;
Though, only because your good side you've shuttered.

When these bad times come
They're sure not to pass right away.
Meanwhile you can mistreat your dog some,
Curtail your oldest and wildest son,
Or be less than complimentary
Of you wife's newest fashion run.

Time, objectiveness
And being with the one you love
Are the very best remedies for your sadness;
With these, sorrow may soon turn to gladness.
True happiness comes from many varied things:
Especially being thankful for whatever you have.

Simple things can ramp up happiness....
A kiss here, a hug there,
A smile from someone new—these
Can turn your sadness to gladness—
And all of a sudden you are a world away
From all this imagined madness.

Lonely Cliff

I'm feeling lonely, so sad and blue,
I need someone; most any girl will do.
Someone to love, to spend life with
And one to end, the peril of this lonely cliff.
Somehow,
I came here so miserable and blue—
Not wanting to endure anymore of it….
Just wanting to split from such mental abuse,
an unfriendly relationship and uselessness..

Finally, I found her who would re-align me
And bring happiness and joy to my front door,
The one who pulled me away from the fatal cliff,
She came around and fixed it all…
Now I have a new life and looking around—
There is a rejoicing, such loving kindness
In the face of it all, thankfully she appeared,
Just someone to share my thoughts to...
Such simple love I was blessed to find
To replace my heartache and feeling down.
I can walk away from this sad open space
And this lonely gap in my life
There's new hope with my new wife—
Diana Jo
I'm so glad I met you!
Anywhere, away and always with you….

SUMMARY...
And In the End

In the Final Analysis

THE VIETNAM WAR WAS A horror to many and many died and laid down their lives for their fellow man. Many more were wounded physically and mentally and experienced great difficulty re-entering society and trying to make a living and keeping a roof over their heads. We owe much to these men and women and most of my generation know this and rebuke the self-righteous ones who screamed and spit upon soldiers as they returned from overseas and whom sometimes even physically abused them. This wasn't the young soldier's war; it was the politician's war.

Many Americans are smart enough to have some respect for our history. In the beginning, we had good intentions in VietNam. Perhaps Communism was slowed, perhaps a nuclear war with China or Russia or both was averted—we just don't know what could have happened good or bad if the VietNam War did not take place. Perhaps there was divine intervention that kept this war from becoming something even far worse.

The VietNam war years were a tumultuous time. Civil rights, anti war demonstrations, the Weather Underground, the violence on the streets and the turmoil of the Democratic Convention gave definition to this decade. A generation of Woodstock youth wanting to get away from it all, found hope and a musical respite from the war's unsettling effects. We excelled in outer space—landing and walking on the Moon's barren surface—yet we could not foresee what chaos a war in SouthEast Asia would bring us.

What started out as an honorable effort to confront, slow, or stop Communist aggression and the fear of a "Domino Effect" theory where one nation in SouthEast Asia after another—would succumb to Communism—turned into a nightmare. Confusion, chaos and flying accusations of political malfeasance grew daily as anti-war protesters organized themselves. Violence soon erupted on the campus lawns and streets of America. The Kent State massacre shone a light on exactly where we were as a nation.

The leaders of China's totalitarian regime had already enslaved about a billion people and stripped them of their freedom and was now supporting Ho Chi Minh's effort to communize South Viet Nam as their next building block.

America's effort after a few years turned into a quagmire of unsustainable jungle warfare that we were not sufficiently prepared for. Our leaders lack of resolve to take the fight to North VietNam amidst all the mounting lives lost and their inability to envision a plan of victory, gave birth to a great abandonment of military purpose.

With twenty thousand troops or more lost by 1967—we became a lost and divided nation. So many fine young men and women had given their lives and futures to keep America free, but our servicemen and women found themselves targeted as monsters of evil as the war dragged on. When it became clear we could not or would not win the war, people like John Kerry and other anti-establishment, anti-war protesters labeled our soldiers as murderous barbarians resembling Genghis Khan. Our military men were portrayed as baby killers after the Mai Lai massacre and the average grunt and Marine in the field became disillusioned and demoralized wondering why our leaders had no solutions to win the war or wind it down and end it. Frustration and anger became rampant among troops and day after day it became harder for them to function. The carpet bombing of the North by our B-52s and the incursions into Laos and Cambodia were of little lasting effect and nothing was working for Richard Nixon and those who had replaced Lyndon Johnson's crew.

American history is unknown or unappreciated by many younger Americans today who should be thankful for their freedom but are not always so and who have not studied the VietNam War era. However, the loss of life and the bloodshed and the sacrifices of our military has been substantial and devastating throughout our brief history of less than 300 years as a nation: and cannot be denied. Through our founding and early revolutionary years and conflicts: through the Civil War, WWI, WWII, Korea, VietNam and recent conflicts in the Middle East—our military men's determination and bloodshed and suffering of the highest magnitude has allowed the United States of America to remain a free Country—free of dictators, free of Socialism, free of Communism, free to excel as individuals however we see fit.

Despite these facts, many Americans, young and old alike, disavow our blood sacrificing campaigns to remain free and refuse to give any thanks or appreciation to our fallen soldiers and their families. Today's leftist universities are not teaching our children—our sons and our daughters—respect for the history of our freedom loving country and instead seek to place a stigma on veterans and all things military. Despite all the hard lessons of history, today's professors and most of those in the media choose to promote a socialist Utopian agenda. They view the world from a globalist perspective where every country is equal despite and absent any regard to the human rights of its citizens and despite a lacking moral fiber that many countries abound in. To many of the political elite (def. those considering themselves to be of a higher regard—at least to themselves) in America and around the world, America is just another country and we are nothing special. These leftists or socialists seek power over the Godly nation of America and show no respect for our past sacrifices to remain free and to help others to remain free. And they are offended by any phrase such as—"America First" and recognize no positive intrinsic value associated with America.

We freed the people behind the "Iron Curtain" and we freed the Jews from Hitler's death camps and we freed people all over Europe in WWII. Socialism and Communism brought all this upon us; what is the reason for any respect for leftist policies above the tenets of our free society in today's world? History has proven over and over again that socialism removes freedom and incentives. America produces wealth and voluntary sharing which makes for a better life for all citizens. Our form of government and free enterprise may not be without faults, but history has shown that a better system has never existed.

We learned that the most powerful nation and military on earth could be beaten up badly by a lesser foe when the battlefield was not well defined.

We also learned that when rules of engagement were constrained and some areas of attack were off limits, and when the enemy had no regard for the lives of their own troops: hard lessons were learned. The strategy of using minimum force to reduce the number of civilian casualties and other such restraining rules of engagement was a conundrum that had to be dealt with. Minimum force was an area that needed much more thought and planning given to it.

Use of nuclear weapons was not to be an asset that could be used in the VietNam War theater and especially against such a small nation and country. Our fear of a nuclear war with China toppled any advantage or leverage that we could have used against China to stop their supply and lifeline to Ho Chi Minh. It had been decided that to stop the "Domino Effect" in VietNam was not worth a nuclear war and this was a very limiting position to be in. In review, we became aware that advance planning and strategy for this type of war had to be different. We learned that our resolve to win at any cost could not be downplayed and that we needed to avoid a conflict if our resolve and the threat against us was an unknown commodity. We learned that we must know our enemy and not assume our warriors could not be outdone or beaten into submission because every conflict is different. We learned without unwavering public support back home that eventually soldier moral would deteriorate to the point that fragging officers occurred.

We learned much about war that would help us in future battles and confrontations. Above all, we learned not to be overconfident and arrogant in our self-image as the most powerful nation on earth. The restraint that we posed on our military men was a bad formula for winning this guerrilla war and it put our soldiers in such an untenable position. So, in summary, all was not lost in VietNam, but the legacy is a very painful one indeed.

the long Black Wall

Have you not seen it?
have you not been there?
isolated and on a downward slope
as we walk on this L shaped mall
it juts out to wake us up
to war and hell's darkest hole—
this long black granite Wall.

A remembrance of an eerie pall,
these names, thereof, are of us all….
they fought and died that we night survive,
that our children might yet live
free of the hellish bondage
of a communism from within
the regions of darkness down below.

We walk down the slope and admire each name;
men and women that decided to fight for what's right,
the veteran, who died that we might live.
So many names looking out at people who walk by;
we stop and linger to read the story of where we've been….
tears flow here and there—imprints of cherished names—
respect and sorrow abounds for the memories of these brave men.

This Viet Nam War Memorial Wall
sheds light on a commitment against socialist sin—
the names of these men who died painfully for us
suffering through the darkest of nights
and we know they would do it again.

The Wall slopes gently and is artistically made,
aesthetically profound and solid in the ground,
its surface beams glowing in the sunlight and
slowly it grows lengthwise out of this sacred ground.

Fifty-eight thousand gone, no more to be seen,
and more and more wounded and MIA;
families shattered, discarded and left so alone
where is our heart located in this matter?

The devil will come again to kill us all,
who will defend our liberty now and then?
he knows he has but a short while
to deceive, deny, accuse and growl.

Where are we when this cloud comes neigh?
will we need another long black memorial Wall
or, will it merely be the downfall and death of us all?
our children are waiting for us to make the call.

History is before us and we need to stand tall,
you've heard, freedom isn't and never has been free....
now, the devil is still lurking to take everything we have—
the scripture is before us if anyone wants to believe....

Many look but don't want to see our destiny,
we are back in the Garden of Eden looking at trees;
with knowledge increased—every last one of us should
bend a knee—are we looking at the wrong tree?

Only God's grace can set us free....
this wall is a statement, a glory to Him

from you and from me and from these three men;
nurses too who served next to these men.

Please, God, forgive us
don't let history repeat us
let us stand and fight to win
so the devil can't come again and again.

www.ingramcontent.com/pod-product-compliance
Lightning Source LLC
Chambersburg PA
CBHW021408290426
44108CB00010B/431